MONEY: 127 Answers

to your most-asked financial questions

**The Q & A reference for everything from
Asset Allocation to Zero-Coupon Bonds**

By Steven C. Camp

TRUNKEY PUBLISHING COMPANY

Cataloging-in-Publication Data

332.024 Camp, Steven C., 1941-
CAM   Money : 127 answers to your most-asked financial questions : a Q & A
         reference for everything from asset allocation to zero-coupon bonds / by
         Steven C. Camp. - Fort Lauderdale, Fl. : Trunkey Publishing Co., © 1995.

         121 p. ; 21 cm.
         Includes index.

         Summary: Provides answers to a multitude of financial questions and gives
         explanations to help readers make smarter money decisions with confidence.

         ISBN 1-887620-00-1 (pbk.)
         95-61186

         1. Finance, Personal - Questions and answers I. Title

                                                              332.024 dc20
                                                              HG179

              Provided in cooperation with Unique Books, Inc.

MONEY:
127 Answers to your most-asked financial questions

Copyright © by Steven C. Camp
ISBN: 1-887620-00-1
Library of Congress Card No.: 95-61186

Published by
Trunkey Publishing Company
2841 NE 21st Court
Fort Lauderdale, FL 33305-3617

Printed in the United States of America

DEDICATION

To the memory of my parents, Lilo and Erwin Camp.

To my wife, Melanie, and our daughters, Elizabeth and Stephanie, for their love, support and assistance. This book was definitely our family project.

To the hundreds of individuals who attended my Informed Investor Seminars. Their questions formed the basis of this book.

Acknowledgments

For publicizing and arranging Informed Investor Seminars at bookstores and libraries in south Florida: Conrad Adelman, Peter Bernard, Tara Brock, Georgina Cardenas, Judy Degraci, Joe Donzelli, Cathy Dube, Deborah Greene, Bob Elkinson, Jamie Forrester, Sherry Friedlander, Jack Holtsberg, Dawn Hyde, Robin Lavine, Judy Martin, Merrill Martin, Moira Novak, Charles Rabin, John Rowe, Jim Rosetti, Dawn Seaman, Stephanie Silton, Tanya Simons-Oprah, Carol Stein, Bob Weaver, Myra Weaver, Susan Yarab, Barbara Young and Nancy Zuckerman.

At a meeting of the Florida Chapter of National Speakers Association, guest speaker, Joe Sabah of Denver, Colorado, suggested that I write this book and encouraged me to get started.

I wish to acknowledge our editor, Ellen Guest of New York. Her suggestions were invaluable in transforming manuscript notes into book form.

Rosalind Sedacca and Richard Munson were responsible for the creative efforts in designing the eye-catching cover and collateral materials.

Special thanks to my associates, Chris Miller, Andrew Molot, Jesus Romero, John H. Rottner, Jeff Sills, Rick Silverman and Sandy Stern for checking the accuracy of the contents. Florence Chester, Ron Halle, Beatrice Huttner, Ralph Leach, Susan Ledbetter, Virginia Levy, Nancy Lucas, Gene Smith, Murray Strongwater and Rhonda Thomasson for providing objective feedback from an investor's point of view.

Readers are encouraged to contact the author with comments and questions.

Steven C. Camp
P. O. Box 11779
Fort Lauderdale, Florida 33339-9930
Telephone: (954) 561-6515
Fax: (954) 561-6569
e-mail: Money 127@aol.com

Introduction

Dear Investor:

As a financial consultant who has conducted numerous public seminars during the past year in south Florida, I was surprised to discover a common need among investors that is not being well addressed. It's a need for basic information about financial planning and investing.

When I conduct seminars, I begin by asking everyone to tell me the questions they would most like answered. This book is made up of more than one hundred of those questions.

My clients know I believe strongly that being an informed investor is crucial to long-term financial success. I also recommend that investors work with a professional financial consultant. Together, you make a team dedicated to a single mission: defining your specific financial goals and then achieving them. But remember: *nobody cares about your money as much as you do.* You need to become an educated investor if you wish to attain your long-term financial goals.

This book will help get you started. My purpose here is not to cover every aspect of investing the way an encyclopedia might. There are other books on the market that do just that. What I want to do is provide some basic information about the kind of real, day-to-day questions concerning money that you and I face again and again. You'll also learn who I recommend that you read in the press and watch on television to keep and stay informed.

After reading through these pages, you may very well find that you have a question about something I haven't covered. *I invite you to communicate directly with me.* I'll try to answer your questions promptly to the best of my ability. My telephone number is (954) 561-6515.

Wishing you a prosperous future.

Steven C. Camp

"After deep meditation I've decided that there can be no inner peace without financial security."

(From the Wall Street Journal — Permission, Cartoon Features Syndicate)

Contents

Contents

Q & A's

Chapter 1 Evaluating Investments

1. Selecting best investment choices
2. Diversification can be duplication
3. Measuring risk when evaluating investment
4. Difference between volatility and risk
5. Stocks or bonds, which are safer?
6. Maintaining income without losing purchasing power during retirement
7. Explanation of asset allocation
8. Difference between rate-of-return and real rate-of-return
9. Point of diminishing returns by being diversified
10. Difference between closed-end and open-end funds
11. Avoiding fees by investing in no-load funds
12. Difference between global and international funds
13. Investing overseas in developed v. emerging markets
14. Dow Jones Industrials percentage of foreign sales
15. Comparative returns of mutual funds load v. no-load
16. Understanding contrarian investment philosophy
17. Investing in commodities
18. Investing in derivatives
19. Suggestions when you win lottery
20. Do your inactive investment accounts managed by Bank Trust Department justify fees charged?
21. Amount of cash reserves needed by 63 year old
22. Explanation of "Rule of 72" of investments doubling

Chapter 2 Brokerage Firms

23. Finding a good broker
24. Suggestions for understanding your brokerage account statements
25. Protection from rogue broker
26. Eliminating annoying sales solicitation telephone calls

Chapter 3 Economic Influences

Chapter 1

Evaluating Investments

Structuring an investment portfolio is an individual matter. Each investor has his or her own unique financial goals, tolerance for risk, time frame, investment experience, and different amount of money he or she wishes to commit. Your portfolio should be the product of a well-executed investment plan that you've reached by consulting with professionals who are thoroughly familiar with your personal circumstances and expectations.

Many of the questions and concerns voiced at my "Informed Investor" seminars deal with the exasperation of investors who are attempting to structure their portfolios. The source of this frustration is the vast number of options investors must choose from. However, by managing risk through diversification and asset allocation, and by maintaining a long-term perspective while still focusing on short-term needs, your investment journey will be smoother and less stressful. And, when you look back after reaching your goal, the trip will have been worth it.

What are your most important long-range goals? Building wealth? Total financial independence? Planning for retirement or college for your children and grandchildren? As your personal situation changes, so may your investment objectives. Realize that you are the author of your plan for financial security, and you can modify this plan as your long-term prospects change.

1

With all these different investment choices available, how can I select the best one?

First determine how much money you need to accumulate by a certain date to accomplish your financial goal. Don't forget to factor in a certain rate for inflation. Based upon your time horizon and tolerance for risk, you will be able to narrow your investment choices and select those with which you are most comfortable. A competent investment adviser, financial planner or broker should be able to suggest suitable investments.

2

I understand the need to be diversified. I'm invested in four different mutual funds. Is this being diversified?

It may not be. Many times individuals invest in three different diversified funds hoping that these funds will provide the variety they need to spread their risk, but upon careful examination, we can see that the major holdings of each of these funds is practically identical. So in the guise of diversifying they have triplicated their portfolios and not really achieved their goal. Diversification means not putting all of your investment eggs in one basket. If the basket falls, you've not only lost your investments, but also the time benefit of compounding.

3

How do I measure risk when evaluating an investment?

There are major causes of risk.

Volatility is a sudden shift in value from high to low or from low to high. The more volatile an investment is, the greater profit you can earn. That's because there is a bigger potential spread between the price you pay for it and its market price when you sell it.

Demanding high yield — When the economy is down and interest rates decline, many investors still expect the same rate of return, and seek therefore investments of lesser quality in order to achieve it. Seeking a higher return can result in higher losses as well.

Playing it too safe — The more money you have in the safest investments (like CDs, bank accounts, and treasury bills), the smaller your chances are for substantial rewards. When you play it too safe, there is always the risk of outliving your assets because they won't keep up with inflation.

4

Are volatility and risk the same?

No. **Volatility** is a two-way street. A volatile investment tends to go up or down more than the market as a whole does. Examples of possible volatile investments are long-term treasury bonds or zero-coupon bonds. As interest rates rise, the value of these investments will decrease. As interest rates drop, the value goes up. Market risk is the downside of volatility.

Liquidity risk is a concern for an investor who is planning to use the proceeds of the sale of an investment for another purpose (paying for a child's tuition, his/her income taxes, the closing costs of a new residence, etc.).

Almost all of us have seen the effects of liquidity risk among people who have lost their jobs, been faced with divorces, or need to relocate when there seems to be no market for their current homes.

5

Am I better off investing in stocks or bonds? Which is safer?

It depends upon your investment objectives — whether you are looking for short-term or long-term gains. If you look at the chart provided by Ibbotson Associates, you will see the performance of stocks and bonds over a 50-year period. Obviously, stocks have done much better.

Which are safer? Bonds used to be safer than stocks; but in 1994, the volatility of the bond market made bond funds less safe than stock funds.

6

As a retiree, how can I maintain my income without losing purchasing power?

This is a dilemma confronting many retirees. Do you realize that, considering today's increasing life spans, you can spend more time being retired than you spent working? If we look at the Ibbotson chart and we see the different performance of stocks, bonds, and Treasury bills over 50 years, we realize that retirees who put their savings in bonds will lose a lot of their purchasing power and will not be able to keep up with inflation. So you need to anticipate not only income needs but also growth needs. That way, your portfolio will grow faster than the rate of inflation, and you will be able to maintain your purchasing power during retirement without being in danger of outliving your savings.

Compound Annual Rate of Return, 1945 - 1995

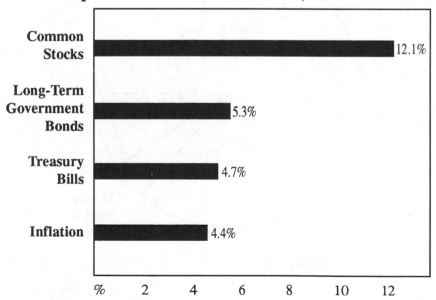

Source: Stocks, Bonds, Bill and Inflation 1995 Yearbook. Ibbotson Associates, Chicago (annually updates by Roger Ibbotson and Rex A. Sinquefield). Used with permission. All rights reserved.

7

Can you explain "asset allocation?"

"Asset allocation" is the process of determining which classes of assets to invest in. For example, you may invest 50% in stocks, 25% in bonds, and 25% in cash money market, so the asset allocation would be referred to as #"50, 25, 25." The way you allocate your assets determines the return over the long run for your individual portfolio. In 91% of all cases, asset allocation was the key influence on portfolio returns.

Components of Investment Return

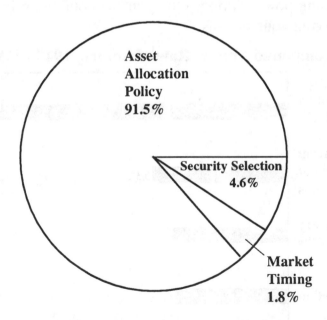

8

What is the difference between rate-of-return and real rate-of-return?

As an investor, the true test is not what you make on your investments but what you get to keep after inflation and taxes. Let's assume you have invested in CD that is returning 5.5%. What is your real rate of return?

Total return	=	5.50%
less 28% Fed. tax	=	-1.54%
less Inflation	=	-4.00%
Real rate of return	=	- .04%

9

You mentioned the need to be diversified in order to minimize risk. How many stocks do I need to own to achieve diversity?

Although that answer will be different for every investor, the benefits of diversification level off when there are more than ten stocks in a portfolio. Take a look at this diagram:

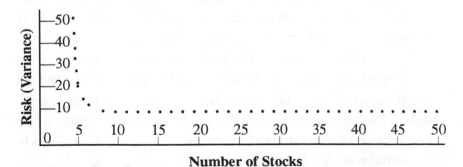

10

What is the difference between closed-end and open-end funds? Which is better?

Open-end funds and closed-end funds are both mutual funds. Open-end funds issue more shares when shares are purchased. When shares are cashed in or sold, open-end funds redeem these shares and then cancel them. Closed-end funds have initial offerings of a limited number of shares. It's very similar to a stock issue; there are a limited number of shares. The price is determined solely by the market. The price of closed-end funds can be more or less than the net asset value.

Which is better? It depends upon your objectives. Usually a closed-end fund invests in a specific sector (such as country funds). With open-end mutual funds, you can transfer from one fund to another within a family of funds without incurring a sales charge.

11

Isn't it cheaper to buy no-load mutual funds because you don't have to pay any fees?

It's a misconception that "no-load" means "no fees," even though many no-load mutual funds maintain toll-free numbers for shareholders and produce elegant brochures. The cost for these services is paid by shareholders in fees. The "no-load" refers to the no-sales load or sales commissions.

Historically, no-load mutual fund shareholders tend to switch out of these funds more quickly than owners of "load" funds. This is because the sales charge acts as an incentive not to bail out at the first market downturn. No-load mutual funds have a much higher redemption rate than "load" mutual funds.

When investors start to try to time the market, they usually penalize themselves by buying high and selling low.

Most investors are better off buying a mutual fund and holding it for the long-run, rather than redeeming it at a downturn and buying more at the upturn.

12

Is there a difference between global funds and international funds?

Yes. Global fund managers invest in stocks of companies throughout the world — including those of the United States. International fund managers invest in stocks of companies outside of the United States or its domestic economy.

More and more, we hear about America being part of the global economy, and about American workers and firms having to compete in the global economy. U.S. businesses, both small and large, have been adapting to this global economy by restructuring their assets, personnel and marketing focuses. Many American companies and brands are globally accepted by consumers worldwide.

In the same way, many foreign companies have plants in the United States and their products are widely accepted by American consumers.

The world is becoming smaller through a global economy that provides mutual benefits through increased trade and improved standards of living. Nowadays, nations have more of an incentive to get along economically, and therefore need to maintain harmonious relations. Can you imagine a business offending or upsetting an important customer? The same holds true for nations dependent upon each other for their economic well-being.

13

To diversify my portfolio through overseas investments, which do you recommend: developed markets like Western Europe and Japan or emerging markets such as those in Latin America and Asia?

According to Morgan Stanley, the annual average rate of return for 1940-1993 was 17% in emerging markets and only 13% in developed markets. The highest growth rates are found in emerging markets. The P/E (price-earnings) ratio is generally lower in emerging markets (reflecting a better value).

I suggest you consult your financial advisor about investing in an emerging market fund with a solid track record. Some of the possible risks of investing in emerging markets that are not encountered in U.S. funds are: fluctuation in currencies, restrictions on foreign investment, the possibility of exchange controls, less publicly available data, less liquidity, and differences in government regulation and supervision. There also may be concerns about political instability, hyperinflation, and market instability.

14

I've heard a lot about the attractive returns from overseas investing, but it sounds risky. Can I benefit from overseas investing by buying stock in blue chip American companies?

Yes. Foreign sales represent approximately an average of 41% of total sales for the thirty companies comprising the Dow Jones Industrial Average (shown below).

The percentage of sales from international sources ranges from a low of 2% for Bethlehem Steel to 79% for Exxon.

The source for these figures is each company's Investor Relations, Media or Public Relations Department and their annual reports. These figures represent the most recent data available as of April 1, 1995.

Company	Stock Symbol	Percentage of International Sales
AT&T	T	25%
Allied Signal	ALD	38%
Alcoa	AA	44%
American Express	AXP	29%
Bethlehem Steel	BS	2%
Boeing	BA	54%
Caterpillar	CAT	49%
Chevron	CHV	28%
Coca-Cola	KO	68%
Disney	DIS	19%
DuPont	DD	47%
Eastman Kodak	EK	53%
Exxon	XON	79%
General Electric	GE	33%
General Motors	GM	28%
Goodyear	GT	42%
IBM	IBM	59%
International Paper	IP	30%
McDonalds	MCD	50%
Merck	MRK	32%
3M	MMM	50%
JP Morgan	JPM	52%
Philip Morris	MO	43%
Proctor Gamble	PG	53%
Sears	S	11%
Texaco	TX	49%
Union Carbide	UK	39%
United Technologies	UTX	54%
Westinghouse	WX	29%
Woolworth	Z	42%

Average International Sales 41%

15

Won't I get a better return by investing in a no-load mutual fund since I will not be charged a sales commission?

A study of investor behavior was conducted by DALBAR Financial Services of Boston and published in April, 1994. DALBAR studied 1,000 mutual fund investors for almost ten years. (This is called the Quantitative Analysis of Investor Behavior.) DALBAR measured the average returns that these 1,000 investors received to determine if investors who pay a sales load and receive advice from a financial consultant, enjoyed better, the same or worse returns than no-load investors do. DALBAR's findings were:

1.   Equity mutual fund investors who used a financial consultant outperformed no-load investors by 19%.
2.   Fixed-income fund investors who used a financial consultant outperformed no-load investors by 17%.

According to DALBAR, "investors who do not seek advice were more likely to panic and sell when the market dived. With the advice and knowledge of a financial consultant available when market conditions are volatile, clients were more likely to hold on to their investments during market downturns."

Many investors who claim to be long-term investors sell at the first downturn. Without someone steady to reassure them that this negative situation is only temporary, investors do not reap the benefit of stable, long-term investments.

16

What is the "contrarian" investment philosophy?

When everyone else seems to look with disfavor upon an investment, contrarians start to buy it. In order to "buy low, sell high" you have to buy in adverse times and sell in robust times. When a company reports disappointing earnings (causing investors to dump a stock), contrarians view this unfavorable event as a buying opportunity.

17

What about investing in commodities?

If you are able to invest in high risk investments such as commodities and can afford to lose the money without it affecting you, your lifestyle, or your retirement plan, then go ahead and invest in high risk investments. But if you can't afford to lose any principal or find it too stressful to lose money, then do not invest in high risk investments such as commodities or options.

18

What are derivatives? Are they a good investment?

Derivatives are financial investments whose value is derived from another security. An option is one type of derivative. The value of an option is derived from the value of the underlying stock. A derivative enables the investor to have considerable leverage. By investing in derivatives, the returns are much greater in up-markets, but the risks are also worse in a down market. But leverage works both ways. When the markets go down, you can lose everything very quickly.

Many professional investors who have been very successful in good times incurred major losses when the market turned against them, because they invested in derivatives. Remember: *"There is no free lunch."* There is a definite relationship between risk and reward.

19

Any suggestions for a person who wins the lottery?

First of all, it is vital that you tell no one of your winnings, because your life will change dramatically and immediately if you do. You will most likely be besieged by people soliciting you for causes and investments you never dreamed of. By maintaining an extremely low profile, you can avoid being taken advantage of.

Another good idea is to change your telephone number and have it unlisted. Meet with an attorney as soon as possible and set up a trust agreement or partnership so that you can minimize the tax effects of receiving a large sum of money. Do not sign the winning ticket until after you have met with your attorney because there can only be one name on the winning ticket. It may be advisable to name as the winner a trust or partnership suggested by your attorney.

It is vital for you to meet with some professionals so that you make the right moves with your new-found wealth. If you have a winning lottery ticket, it is essential that you safeguard it. Put it in a safe place and tell only those you trust of its location.

There was a $17+ million lottery winner in Melbourne, Florida, on Sept. 4, 1993. She owned a local beauty salon and her husband was an air force sergeant. This woman told no one about her winning ticket, not even her spouse or grown children. She put it in a bank safe deposit for safekeeping. At Christmas, she gave her husband a gift-wrapped present containing this winning ticket. But that could have been a big mistake. If she had become ill or incapacitated, the expiration date could have passed (six months and one day after the date on that winning ticket) and the ticket would have become worthless.

In 1994, more than 120 people were struck by lightning in Florida and less than 40 people won the lottery. A Florida resident has more than a three-times-greater chance of being struck by lightning than winning the lottery.

20

I have an investment account managed by the trust department of a major bank. Most of my assets are in municipal bonds, and the rest is in stocks that I've owned for many years. I cannot afford to sell them because of the capital gains taxes that I would have to pay. Should I maintain this account even though I have to pay approximately one percent on the value of my assets in this account annually, and also approximately one percent on any income I receive from this account?

If you are maintaining an investment account at the trust department of a bank and the account is being warehoused or stored, you may want to reevaluate the account's cost structure with the person handling your account at the bank. You may be in an excellent position to renegotiate your fee structure if there are no transactions within your account and your account is static. That same account in a brokerage firm would not be charged a set percentage fee just to store municipal bonds and securities.

21

How much do you recommend I maintain in cash for quick access? I am 63 years old.

A good rule-of-thumb is to maintain three to six months' worth of living expenses in cash or money market funds. As one becomes older, there is a tendency to maintain larger amounts in cash. You should maintain an amount that you feel comfortable having in cash. Some retirees take this to an extreme and maintain two to three years' worth of living expenses in cash or money market. It's probably not a good idea to maintain this much money in cash or money market funds because it will not grow as fast as the rate of inflation.

22

Could you explain the "Rule of 72?"

The "Rule of 72" is used by investors to compute the amount of time it will take for an investment to double in value. If you take the rate of return you want and divide it into the number 72, the result will be the number of years it takes for the investment to double. For example, if you assume an investment will have an 8% rate of return (compounded annually), divide 72 by 8. Since 72 divided by 8 equals nine, it will take approximately nine years for that investment to double.

If you divide the number of years it takes for an investment to double into 72, you will get the compounded annual rate of return. For example, if you could double an investment in five years, and you divide five into 72, the result is about 14 plus percent (compounded annually). This is the "Rule of 72." Many people are fascinated by this rule. It works in the same way that 3.14 (pi) works in computing the area or circumference of a circle.

Chapter 2

Brokerage Firms

Most Americans feel financial pressures from all sides and must also feel that their personal financial situations have not improved during the past five years. Its also true that most Americans do not have clear financial plans. By developing a realistic financial plan and paying yourself first, you will be in a better position to achieve your goals. Seek the assistance of a competent financial professional to advise you on investment choices that suit your expectations and tolerance for risk.

Since I am associated with a major brokerage firm, many of the questions asked at my seminars are about whether or not to have a broker, how to find a "good broker," the problems that may occur if your broker goes out of business, and the ways an investor can use the professional services of a brokerage firm.

When you visit your accountant or tax-preparer, what type

of client are you?

*Do you drop off a shoe box or shopping bag full of last
year's receipts with the expectation that they will be sorted,
compiled and used in preparing your tax returns?*
or
*Do you have last year's income and expense files neatly
prepared and documented so that your records are easy to follow and self explanatory?*

Many people realize that they have neither the time, energy, inclination nor financial expertise to act as money-man-
agers. They seek the services of a professional. These investors are not giving up control of their investments; they are
using a broker as a financial consultant or investment advisor.
In this age of specialization, it usually pays to "do what you do
best and hire out the rest." Successful people know how to use
"OPB" ("other people's brains"). If you are a biologist, automobile dealer, orchestra cellist or realtor, then how are you
going to find the time, money and energy to be a do-it-your-
self money manager?

23

How do you find a good broker?

Much the same way you'd find a good lawyer, a good
accountant, a good doctor, or a good mechanic. Ask friends,
and people whom you trust. Find out what they value about
that person, and use that as the basis for making your decision.
Then meet with that person and discover if he or she is com-
patible with you. Does his or her viewpoint of the economy
and market make sense to you? Does he or she understand
your risk tolerance? Your investment objectives? Are the lev-

els of expectations for each of you in harmony? Also, does he or she fully answer the questions that you ask? Is that person condescending or patronizing to you? If so, you will want to work with someone else.

24

I get a monthly brokerage account statement and I do not know how to read it. What suggestions do you have for helping me to understand my statement?

Many clients do not understand their monthly statements and are reluctant to ask for help. (They also may not check their checking account statements from their local banks each month.)

Meet with your financial consultant and have him or her explain your entire brokerage account statement so that you fully understand it. If there is any part of the statement that you don't understand, make sure it is explained to you.

If you are not comfortable approaching your financial consultant, you can speak to his or her customer service assistant and have that person explain it to you. You owe it to yourself to understand the monthly statement from your brokerage firm because you are ultimately responsible for what happens in your account. It's your money!

25

I have an account at a brokerage firm and I like my broker a lot. However, I read stories in the newspapers about brokers embezzling money from their customers. How can I protect myself against being ripped off ?

First, never forget that no one cares about your money as much as you. Get involved in understanding your financial affairs — do not delegate this responsibility completely to a broker, financial advisor, accountant, friend, family member, or even your spouse.

You are responsible for:

1. Reading and understanding your statements, and looking for errors or omissions. Ask your broker or branch operations manager to explain anything you do not understand.

2. Examining your trade confirmations to make sure they are accurate. File your statements in a loose-leaf notebook separated by month or quarter, and look for any changes in security positions.

To check whether a broker has been disciplined by a regulatory agency or by the NASD in the past, call the NASD toll-free hotline at (1-800-289-9999). To find out if the firm is a member of SIPC (Securities Investor Protection Corporation) call SIPC-1-202-371-8300. All brokers and dealers registered with the SEC and with national stock exchanges are required to be members. The SIPC insures customers' accounts in case the firm fails. The overall maximum is $500,000 per customer, with a limit of $100,000 in cash or cash equivalents. In addition to the $500,000 protection, provided by SIPC, some firms provide additional insurance. SIPC does not provide insurance against market risks.

26

I get bombarded with annoying telephone calls from brokers who are trying to sell me the latest stock or bond of the day. They usually call around dinner time. Is there anything I can do to be removed from these cold-calling lists?

Yes, there is. For instance, if you live in Florida and don't wish to receive sales solicitation calls, get your name added to the "No Sales Solicitation Calls" list maintained by the Florida Department of Consumer Services. (Call the Division of Consumer Services at 1-800-HELP-FLA.) The list is updated quarterly. Your number will remain on the list for one year. The one-year fee is $5. Businesses that solicit calls from numbers on this list can be fined $10,000.

In other states, call the State Attorney General's office or the Department of Consumer Affairs.

27

What are the pros and cons of placing my securities in a brokerage firm's vault versus keeping them in my safe deposit box?

Many people are reluctant to put securities in a brokerage firm's vault. By leaving them in their own safe deposit boxes, they feel they're safer and under their own control. Unfortunately, many securities are misplaced this way. And if you ever lose a stock certificate or a bond, it is a problem to replace it. Also, if you become incapacitated, ill, or die, then access to the securities in the safe deposit box may become very difficult — or even denied — in certain states.

Securities placed in a brokerage firm's vault are insured by SIPC (Securities Investor Protection Corporation) for up to

$500,000. Some firms also carry additional insurance for their clients' accounts.

Securities held at a brokerage firm are probably safer and easier to track than securities held in a safe deposit box.

Many retirees are not enjoying their retirements because they are spending 2-3 or more hours daily managing their investments. Much unnecessary paperwork could easily be computerized and done more accurately by a brokerage firm.

28

What is the difference between the prime rate and the discount rate? Or are they the same?

No. They're not the same. The discount rate is the interest rate that the Federal Reserve charges member banks when those banks borrow money using government securities as collateral. The raising or lowering of the discount rate is one of the tools the Federal Reserve has to try to stimulate the economy or to reduce inflationary pressures.

The prime rate is the interest rate that banks charge for loans to their most creditworthy customers. It is considered a key benchmark because other rates are tied into it. For example, the interest rate for many credit cards (home equity loan and automobile leases) is based upon the prime rate plus a set number of percentage points.

29

What happens if my broker becomes bankrupt? Are my securities protected?

If your brokerage firm is a member of the Securities Investors Protection Corporation (SIPC), the account is insured for balances up to $500,000.

Ask your broker for information.

30

How would you describe an ideal investor or client?

An ideal investor does five things:

1. Is willing to invest without procrastinating.
2. Consistently adds to his/her account.
3. Communicates clearly his/her risk tolerance, and has reasonable expectations.
4. Expects the market to fluctuate, and takes advantage of any fluctuations via dollar cost averaging.
5. Doesn't get discouraged when things get tough. That means having the long-term perspective to ride the ups and downs of the market, and doesn't sell at the first down-turn.

31

How can I be more knowledgeable about investing so I don't need a broker?

Without being facetious, all you need to do is have as much knowledge, judgment, and up-to-date information as a competent full-time broker or adviser. In addition, you need to be willing and able to spend 40-50 hours weekly managing and monitoring your investments.

Obviously, if you're asking this question, you have reason to feel that the commissions you have paid in the past to a brokerage firm or broker have not been justly earned by that broker or firm.

32

How do I calculate my net worth?

Your net worth is a balance sheet listing of your assets (what you own) and your liabilities (what you owe). The difference represents your net worth.

Your bank can give you a "Statement of Net Worth" form that is used by loan applicants. Fill in values for assets using the appropriate market value (not your cost price). Separate your assets by liquid and non-liquid investments. (Retirement plan assets such as 401(k) plans are considered non-liquid assets.)

33

What kind of questions should my financial advisor be asking me when we meet for the first time? What should I tell him or her?

Some of the questions your financial advisor should be asking deal with your objectives for investing: the reasons why you are investing, the level of risk that you are able to assume, and the amount of money you have to invest. Remember that your financial advisor is a consultant. In order to help you, he or she needs as much information as possible about your expectations, your prior investment experience, your assets and liabilities, and your time horizon. This person should treat everything you say as confidential — you need to be clear about that with this person before divulging any information. You should tell your financial advisor everything he or she needs to understand about your finances (including your prior investment successes, disappointments and expectations). If you have accounts held at other firms, let this person know. If you or members of your family have any major health or interpersonal problems, your financial advisor may need to know this information. This way he or she will be able to better advise you about health and estate planning matters.

34

How does a discretionary account work?

In a discretionary account, you authorize a financial consultant or broker to make investment decisions without consulting you first. The broker has the authority (or "discretion")to buy or sell investments that he or she thinks are in your best interests.

35

I am 74 years old and have accounts at three brokerage firms. Do you advise that I consolidate these three accounts into one?

I recommend that you do whatever you feel most comfortable doing. If you can manage three different accounts, and each of the accounts is enabling you to achieve your investment objectives, there may be no need to consolidate them. However, many investors who maintain different accounts may be creating a tremendous amount of unnecessary paperwork for themselves.

If you are one of these people, consolidate your investments with the financial advisor with whom you feel most comfortable and believe is most able to help you obtain your objectives. Consolidation of brokerage accounts facilitates timely settlements and helps to prevent late fees and interest charges. Remember, it is important for you to streamline your portfolio and eliminate unnecessary paperwork while you're in good health. Can you imagine the hassles and added expenses that your loved ones will have trying to unravel your affairs if you are not able to help them?

Chapter 3

Economic Influences

It is estimated that two thirds of all Americans do not pay their Visa or Mastercard bills in full when they receive them. Many simply make the minimum payment and let the annual interest charges of 18% plus escalate.

Interest rate charges for consumer debt are no longer tax deductible. This means that people in the 28% tax bracket must earn 25% before taxes to be able to afford to pay 18% in interest charges after taxes for their credit card debt. Where can you find an investment guaranteed to pay you a 25% annual return? By eliminating your credit card debt you will have avoided a minus 25% annual drain on your assets.

Many investors feel that the greatest risk to their portfolios is economic and financial volatility. It is not. Inflation is the greatest risk.

If inflation averages 4% annually, how much will your purchasing power shrink?

After 5 years of 4% inflation, the value of $1 is just 82 cents
10 years,	the value of $1	66 cents
15 years,	the value of $1	54 cents
20 years,	the value of $1	44 cents
25 years,	the value of $1	36 cents

This means that a 4% annual inflation rate will reduce the purchasing power of $100,000 as follows:

Number of years	Purchasing power
5 years	$82,000
10 years	$66,000
15 years	$54,000
20 years	$44,000
25 years	$36,000
30 years	$30,000

As we examine these figures (assuming that inflation will only average 4% annually), today's retiree will need to double his or her income every 18 years to maintain the same standard of living they currently enjoy.

36

I watch *Wall Street Week* every Friday on PBS and enjoy it. However, I'm totally confused after seeing this panel of experts disagree — some are bearish and others are bullish. Do you have any suggestions for making sense of all of this?

These days we have a surplus of information — and much of that information is contradictory. It is very confusing to hear one expert give cogent reasons for the economy to perform in a certain way and then hear another expert argue forcefully about why the economy is likely to move in the opposite direction. The credentials of each expert are apt to be very impressive, and this only adds to the frustration.

I sympathize. And I am reminded of a recent year-end *Wall Street Week* program. Each of the guests on the show was dressed formally as if he or she were attending a New Year's Eve Party. The host reviewed each of the expert's predictions for the past year and then invited them to predict the highs and lows of the Dow Jones Industrials for the next 12 months. (The variation among the guests in predicting the year-end for the Dow varied by more than 1,000 points.)

We need to keep these short-term views in perspective. The truth is, smart investors take a long-range view and invest for the long-run. If you invest over the long-run in solid companies and solid investments, then the minor ups-and-downs of the market (and of the opinions of commentators) have a minimal impact on your portfolio.

Here are some rules for long-term success: Invest in companies that are leaders in their industries and enjoy a 15% or more annual increase in earnings over the past five years. Reinvest the dividends. Companies that are able to increase their earnings consistently regardless of the economy are usually well-run. Avoid being enticed by "bargains" in the stock market that offer "a quick killing." Review your monthly financial statements, and do not worry about monitoring your investments every day. Remember, you're in it for the long run.

37

Whenever there is a negative economic report (like an increase in unemployment), the stock market seems to go up. Why is bad news good for the stock market?

Wall Street has a tremendous fear of inflation. When reports say that the economy is doing well, analysts fear that the economy will be heating up and that inflation will start to rise. Since that tends to have long-term negative effects upon the stock market, analysts tend to agree that the Federal Reserve will have to step in and raise interest rates. The Fed may also reduce the economy's money supply. This tends to slow the economy and prevent expansion — and can almost create a recession. This has a detrimental effect upon the stock market in the long run.

When there is economic bad news (which indicates that the economy is growing slowly or not at all), then the Federal Reserve is likely to stimulate the economy by encouraging businesses to borrow by lowering interest rates. This has a positive effect upon the stock market.

38

What prompts the Federal Reserve Board to raise or lower interest rates? Are there any indicators that can help individual investors like me anticipate the moves of the Fed?

Fears or concerns about the economy prompts the Federal Reserve to adjust interest rates. Fear of inflation can cause the Fed to raise interest rates, and fear of recession or economic slowdown prompts the Fed to lower interest rates. Some of the indicators you may wish to keep an eye on are:

- **Producer Price Index (PPI)** is an excellent indicator of future price increases or decreases.
- **Consumer Price Indexes (CPI)** is a survey of housing prices, utilities, consumer products and services.
- **Gross Domestic Product** measures growth or business activity. (Generally, when GDP is above 3%, it is considered inflationary.)
- **Capacity Utilization** is a measurement of the rate in which plants and utilities operate as a percent of total capacity.
- **Employment and Unemployment Data.** As employment figures go up, more employment creates more demand for workers. This results in higher wages, which is considered inflationary.

39

What is the "retirement gender gap?"

Very simply, women outlive men, and need their retirement assets to sustain them for six years longer. That's the "retirement gender gap."

According to KPMG Peat Marwick, women over age 25 are employed an average of 4.8 years for every 6.6 years that men work. Frequently, full vesting in corporate pension plans requires five years of continuous employment. Since women tend to earn 63% of the salary of a male colleague, and receive fewer pension benefits, they will be forced to save a greater portion of their incomes in order to have the same standard of living as men do when they retire.

40

I've heard it mentioned that women need to earn higher returns on their investments than men. Why?

Some analysts say that, because women usually earn only 60-70% of what men make, they have to catch up by making sure they earn higher returns on their investments. This may be valid in many situations, and I do not dispute their answer. However, even if we assume there is no difference in pay between genders, women still need to earn a higher return simply because usually they live about six years longer than men do.

According to the National Council for Health Statistics, among all Americans born in 1950 who attain age 65, men are projected to live to age 81 while women are projected to live to age 87. This means that because many women often care for the children, they spend fewer years in the work force and enjoy fewer pension benefits.

41

I'm a recent widow. My husband managed all of our investments for more than fifty years— while I raised our children. I am afraid to manage these investments because I have no experience in financial planning. I can't afford to lose this money. But I also don't want to have to depend upon a stranger for my financial well-being. What should I do?

Many women are in your situation because many women have, historically, married men five to ten years older than themselves. Also, women outlive men by six years on the average. This means that many women are widows for fifteen to twenty years. Many women who are currently in their sixties or seventies never worked outside of their homes. They raised their children while their husbands earned a living and managed the family's investments. They had no preparation, knowledge or experience of financial matters because their husbands took care of everything. Unfortunately, they have no choice now that they are widows. They must assume responsibility because no one else will. *You must recognize that no one is more concerned about your money than you are.*

You can start to become knowledgeable by attending seminars, reading some basic books on investment, or enrolling in a local adult education course. And don't be afraid to ask questions. If you have a relationship with a broker or financial consultant, insist that this person explains everything that you feel you should know about. If you are uncomfortable with anything about an investment, make sure it's clarified to your satisfaction. If you have a broker who wants to take over and asks you to sign a discretionary account, be aware that you are giving that person limited control over your finances.

By having some basic knowledge about investing, you will be able to ask the right questions. You'll feel confident that you are making good decisions about your own well-being, and are not dependent upon others for your financial health.

Let me stress once more the importance of not being afraid to ask a question about your portfolio because you feel "it's a dumb question." The only dumb question is the one you were too embarrassed to ask. Remember, it is your money, so go ahead and ask that question!

42

My son is a sophomore in college. Recently he asked me which career would provide the best job security. What should I tell him?

Tell him that job security is an oxymoron. It is an anachronism not only in America, but also in almost all modern societies. Even U.S. Military and U.S. Naval Academy career officers who were combat veterans in the Persian Gulf are being separated from the service prior to retirement.

The concept of working for one company for 30-40 years and then retiring is outdated. Companies that were known for never laying off employees (like IBM) are using all sorts of euphemisms to verbally soften the impact of firing employees for economic reasons. "Downsizing," "outplacing," "de-jobbing," and "discharging" are some of the terms used.

The dwindling size of Fortune 500 Corporation work forces has motivated many displaced employees to operate small businesses out of their homes. These small businesses are frequently linked electronically (by fax, e-mail, and Internet) which enables these entrepreneurs to benefit from flexible working time and more creative environments. They have been the fuel that's fed our economy's most recent recovery.

What can your son do to prepare himself so that he has job security when he graduates? He must realize that he really is in business for himself, and needs to market himself on a temporary basis to his employer, knowing that his position is temporary. Realizing this temporary state of employment, he must be constantly improving his marketable skills and must always be ready to adapt to changes in the workplace.

Tell your son that he needs to develop public speaking skills, become computer proficient and (especially if he wishes to go into business in an internationally diverse region like California, Arizona, Texas or Florida) be able to speak and understand Spanish. He can learn public speaking at schools or at Toastmasters clubs. Why Spanish? Within 4-5 years, approximately 20% of the U.S. population will speak Spanish as a primary language. Spanish speakers represent one of the fastest growing segments of our population.

43

What will happen when baby boomers begin to retire?

It is estimated that in 2010, when baby boomers start to reach age 65, the number of retirees will soar. During the next decade, the overall population growth in the U.S. is expected to grow at approximately 2% while population growth for retirees is expected to exceed 25%. Currently, about five working Americans support one retiree. When the baby boomers begin to retire, it is estimated that three working Americans will support one retiree.

Reducing Social Security or Medicare benefits is a hot potato that almost all politicians refuse to touch because they fear that retirees in their districts will vote them out of office at the next election if they do take a position.

The more politically palatable remedy will be to increase the age when retirement benefits begin. Complicating this formula are unknowns such as increasing longevity due to medical advances like genetic engineering and discoveries of cures for diseases (especially those affecting the elderly).

If the aging process can be delayed by medical advances and discoveries (as some foresee), the retirement age in 25-40 years may be 75-80 years.

44

How does the stock market perform during pre-election years?

Since 1940, pre-election years have been, by far, the best-performing years for the market. Realizing that past performance is no indication of future results, the numbers for the past 50+ years for the S&P index with dividends reinvested are:

pre-election year average	+21.05%
election year average	+12.40%
post-election year average	+ 7.81%
mid-term election year average	+10.23%

45

What is the NASD?

"NASD" stands for the National Association of Securities Dealers. The NASD operates under the supervision of the Securities and Exchange Commission (SEC), and under fair and equitable rules of securities trading.

46

How does indexing work?

Indexing is a way to remove the effects of inflation when calculating benefits for special groups, or when measuring real results from an investment.

For example, benefits for both Social Security recipients

and military retirees are indexed to the Consumer Price Index (CPI).

By using indexing to compute the real rate of return, some tax reformers suggest that home owners will not be penalized when selling homes that have appreciated solely because of inflation. Others recommend that indexing be used to calculate capital gains for all investments.

47

What is the relationship between the budget deficit, the national debt, and the stock market?

The budget deficit (which is computed annually) is the difference between the amount of receipts and expenditures of our federal budget. (By the way, the sum of the annual budget deficits since this country was founded equals the total national debt of our nation today.)

As the debt service (interest payments to bond holders) of our national debt increases (representing a bigger drain on our economy), the stock market suffers. Currently, one out of six dollars raised in taxes is used to pay interest on our national debt. As this debt increases, we will have less money to pay for capital investment and to rebuild the infrastructure of our country. That threatens to reduce our standard of living, and will certainly depress the stock market.

48

Isn't most of the U.S. national debt in the hands of foreigners?

No. Approximately $750 billion worth of U.S. Treasury bonds are in the hands of foreigners. This figure seems immense, and it is. But it is only 15% of the national debt, which is currently about $5 trillion. The largest holders of the national debt are domestic pension funds.

49

Do you think Social Security will be around when I am ready to retire? I am 29 years old.

A recent survey asked Americans in their 20s — your age group — about their attitude and opinion of Social Security. More of them believed in the existence of UFOs than that they would someday receive Social Security benefits. Social Security will survive — but benefits will probably decrease as older eligibility ages are established. The normal retirement age of 65 years will begin to change in the year 2000. This will affect those born after 1937 and the eligibility age will gradually increase to 67.

You must take responsibility for your retirement by realizing Social Security will provide only a base level of income during your retirement years. It was never intended to function as a retirement plan but only as a supplement. You need to shoulder your retirement needs by starting to invest in tax-deferred investments such as IRAs, 401(k) plan, SEPs, and Keogh when you are young so that time and compound interest will make your retirement nest egg multiply. Never before has a comfortable retirement depended more on personal financial planning and disciplined savings.

50

I've heard the term "sandwich generation." What does it mean?

The "sandwich generation" refers to the generation (usually in their 40s or 50s now), who are supporting elderly parents as well as providing financial support for their children (usually by paying for their college educations). This generation is *sandwiched* between an older and younger generation.

In addition to be sandwiched between parents and their children, many are trying to provide for their own retirements. They may also be faced with the possibility of downsizing within their own companies and are concerned about the possible loss of their livelihoods. All this pressure to balance conflicting demands creates considerable stress. To compound this problem, their adult children may be part of the "baby boomerang" generation. (These are adult children who have left the family nest and later return to live with their parents.)

51

Would you explain the difference between growth stocks and income stocks?

Growth stocks, as their name suggests, offer above-average growth that exceeds the rate of inflation. If you are seeking to benefit from your investments in five years or more and don't need current income, you'll probably benefit more by investing in growth stocks, especially if they are in a tax-sheltered retirement account such as IRA or 401(k) plan.

Income stocks provide relatively high-paying dividends; utilities used to be in this category until 1993-1994. There is a trade off between income and growth. Many retirees in their

60s mistakenly seek to maximize their current returns or current incomes by forsaking growth in their portfolios. These retirees are positioning themselves to be victimized by inflation if they live a normal or longer-than-normal life span.

52

How can I learn more about investing so that I don't have to depend upon others for my financial well-being?

Attend more seminars, enroll in a basic adult education course in your community; get an overview by reading some of the "How to" books in this store or from your local library.

53

Can you recommend any books on investing?

"Making The Most Of Your Money" by Jane Bryant Quinn is an easy-to-follow step-by-step guide about organizing your financial affairs. (You can even learn while commuting; it is available in four audio cassettes which are read by the author.) Ms. Quinn is a columnist for *Newsweek* magazine and is syndicated in 250 newspapers nationwide.

There are many other excellent books on investing, such as Peter Lynch's "Beating The Street." He writes in an easy-to-understand manner, avoids jargon-and makes sense. Mr. Lynch earned his reputation as a manager of the Fidelity Magellan Fund.

Another book is "Stocks for the Long Run: A Guide For Selecting Markets for Long-Term Growth" by Jeremy Siegel, professor of finance at the Wharton School, University of Pennsylvania. The book makes a strong case for investing in stocks rather than bonds over the long run, by showing that a 40-year old saving for retirement can expect much higher returns from stocks than bonds. Dr. Siegel was recently voted "Best Business School Professor" by *Business Week* magazine.

"The Great Boom Ahead" by Harry S. Dent, Jr. is an upbeat forecast for investors on the reasons they will prosper during America's protracted boom. After reading this book I felt very positive about our economy. Dent believes that as the baby boomers reach their peak spending years (ages 45-50), this spending wave will result in a Great Boom. Dent presents a very persuasive case for investing in equities to capitalize on "The Great Boom Ahead."

In addition to reading these books, you may wish to enroll in an adult education course at your local high school or college.

54

Can you recommend some magazines I can read to be better informed about my investments?

A lot depends upon your background, education, investment experience, available time and financial situation.

Some of the magazines to which I subscribe are *Forbes, Fortune, The Economist, Florida Trend, Consumer Reports, US News & World Report, Barron's, South Florida Business Journal, Business in Broward* magazine, *Wharton, Newsweek* and *Bottom Line* newsletter. In addition, I read two local newspapers and *The Wall Street Journal* each morning. At my office, there are company publications that help keep me informed about the markets.

I confess that I am frequently frustrated because I don't have enough time to read all of them.

If you're just starting out and have no prior investment

experience or knowledge, *Kiplinger's Personal Finance* magazine is an excellent choice. I suggest you attend seminars that
are not pushing a specific product, and try watching the CNBC
channel on cable television or the *Nightly Business Report* on
public broadcasting television stations.

Chapter 4

Retirement

In the last decade, we have been forced to assume more and more responsibility for our comfortable retirement as employers have increasingly switched from retirement plans with defined benefits to defined contribution retirement plans. Most of these plans are different than government pensions— they lack cost-of-living adjustments (CO-LAS). Under these plans, you— not your employer— are solely responsible for ensuring that your investments will adequately fund your retirement.

With the average retirement now spanning 20 to 30 years, the major concern for most investors is the danger of outliving one's assets. Taxes have increased and investors are concerned about reduced earnings on their future income. Increased taxes have affected Social Security recipients; 85% of Social Security benefits are currently taxed for retirees with joint incomes of $44,000 or more and individual incomes of $34,000 or more.

The most-asked questions at these seminars at libraries

and book stores are from retirees and pre-retirees. Many are exasperated by the effects of inflation but are too risk-averse to put a major part of their portfolios in investments that normally grow faster than the inflation rate. Playing it too safe by investing in CDs is threatening their purchasing power.

Many brochures printed by banks, mutual fund companies and brokerage firms are entitled "How Can I Afford Retirement?" or "Are You Prepared To Live To Age 85, 90 or 95?" "Are You Saving Enough Or Investing Enough For Retirement?" "Will You Be Able To Afford To Send Your Children To The College Of Their Choice?" One recent ad by a major brokerage firm caught my attention with its dramatic message. "Imagine the cost of putting 15 kids through an Ivy League college and you'll have some idea of what you'll need for a comfortable retirement." By taking advantage of 401(k) and other employee-sponsored plans, you reduce your taxable income by the amount you invest via payroll deductions.

If you are self-employed, take advantage of the benefits of establishing a qualified retirement plan such as an Individual Retirement Account (IRA), Simplified Employee Pension Plan (SEP) or a Keogh Plan.

55

What can I do so that I don't outlive my retirement assets?

This is the #1 concern for most investors. People are living longer and longer, and they're rightly afraid that they might outlive their savings.

To put it in a nutshell, if you can ensure that your retirement assets grow faster than the rate of inflation, then you will never outlive your retirement assets.

One way to ensure that you will not outlive your retirement assets is to have long-term health care insurance, so that your assets are not depleted in order to provide living expenses in case you're ill or incapacitated. You need to get this insurance while you are healthy and insurable.

56

What is the cost of procrastinating in beginning an investment plan?

Many people intend to contribute to their retirement plans or establish a college education for their infant son or daughter but fail to follow through.

The price of this procrastination can be staggering. The chart below shows the difference in growth between an individual who makes a one-time $10,000 contribution to a retirement plan at age 25 and an individual who makes that $10,000 contribution 10 years later, at age 35. (This assumes a tax sheltered investment with an annual rate of 10%.) In addition, the benefits of compounding are severely reduced by procrastinating.

The cost of waiting to invest $10,000:

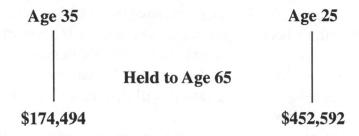

Age 35		**Age 25**
	Held to Age 65	
$174,494		**$452,592**

57

I am 48 years old, self-employed, recently divorced and have been unable to start saving for retirement. Is it too late to start a retirement program?

It's never too late. Many people have been interrupted in their retirement planning due to divorce or loss of a job. Start saving now. If you look at your alternative, you can't afford not to start saving for your retirement.

58

What would happen to my IRA (Individual Retirement Account) if I died before I cashed it in? What about taxes?

After your death, your beneficiary will have several choices for receiving the proceeds from your IRA. The 10% penalty tax doesn't apply to these distributions, regardless of your age or your beneficiary's age. The distribution is subject, however, to income taxes (except for amounts that represent a return of nondeductible contributions). Thus, how your beneficiary elects to receive the proceeds can have a significant effect on the tax bill.

For example, if you had already started taking the required distributions because you were over age 70-1/2, your beneficiary could continue to take periodic distributions on the same schedule. If distributions had not yet begun, the relationship of the beneficiary to the owner will determine how the funds can be withdrawn.

The greatest number of options are available to surviving spouses. Your spouse can cash in all or part of the IRA without paying the 10% penalty. Or your spouse can roll over the IRA to his/her own IRA, making the money subject to the same rules as their own IRA. (Thus he or she would pay a 10% penalty tax if the funds were withdrawn before the age of 59-1/2 and withdrawals must start by age 70-1/2.) Another option is to allow the funds to remain in your IRA. The funds can remain in your IRA until the year you would have turned 70-1/2, at which time your spouse would have to start taking distributions based upon his or her life expectancy.

If your beneficiary is not your spouse, he or she has two basic options. Either funds can be withdrawn from the IRA within five years, or the beneficiary can start to take withdrawals within one year of your death (based upon his or her life expectancy). It is important that you name a beneficiary for your IRA in order to make these options available to your heirs. If you don't have a beneficiary and someone inherits your IRA under a will, their only option is to cash in the entire balance in the IRA within five years.

59

What is a SEP Retirement Plan? Does it require a lot of paperwork to open?

SEP stands for "Simplified Employee Pension Plan" (it is sometimes referred to as a SEP-IRA). A SEP is an employer-sponsored retirement savings program; the paperwork required to open one only consists of a one-page agreement.

SEPs are much less complicated to establish and maintain than traditional pension plans are, and they offer more benefits than a standard IRA. A standard IRA only allows annual tax-deductible contributions of up to $2,000, whereas a SEP permits contributions up to 15% of annual compensation (up to $22,500).

Contributions to a SEP are a tax-deductible expense. Even if you are in a one-man or one-woman business, you're eligible for a SEP.

60

I work for a Fortune 500 company and have enrolled in its 401(k) retirement plan. There are about a half dozen investments for me to choose from. What should I do?

A lot depends upon your investment objectives and your age. If you have five or more years until retirement, you may wish to look for growth. Don't keep most of your money in money market funds, government obligation or bond funds. Rather, invest your money in growth funds (both domestic and international). This will keep you ahead of inflation.

Since there are more than 5,600 mutual funds available on the market today, it is very hard to recommend funds without knowing first which funds are offered on your 401(k) selection menu. But if you do have a financial consultant, let him or her know about your 401(k) plan and ask for recommendations. Even though your consultant does not directly benefit from your 401(k) plan, I believe that he or she will probably extend the courtesy of helping you since you give him other business.

61

As a retiree, how can I maintain my current income (while interest rates are declining) without increasing my risk?

This depends upon what your current investments are. If your current investments are CDs and money market funds, and you wish to increase your return, you will have to increase your risk. There is a strong relationship between risk and reward. You can't avoid some risk of principal if you try to increase your return. However, if you have no risk of principal and your return is less than the rate of inflation, you will lose money each year.

62

We have a 401(k) plan at work and I haven't participated because I just don't understand it. It seems so complicated. Would you explain what a 401(k) plan is and how it works in simple terms so that I can understand it?

A 401(k) plan is a voluntary retirement program sponsored by your employer. It provides you with an opportunity to save for your retirement through payroll deductions, which are made before taxes are withheld. In addition to deferring taxes on the amount of your contributions, the earnings on these amounts will compound even faster than they would otherwise because all taxes are deferred until you start withdrawing them from your 401(k) retirement plan.

Some companies match employee contributions up to a certain amount or percentage. This is an excellent opportunity to double your money instantly. According to *Kiplinger's Personal Finance* magazine, approximately 25% of eligible employees do not participate in their companies' 401(k) plans.

63

If I withdraw funds from my retirement plan, what are the tax consequences?

If you are under age 59 1/2, there is a 10% penalty on the amount withdrawed plus regular income tax on the amount withdrawn. In addition to the tax consequences, premature withdrawals from investments earmarked to provide for your retirement deny you the benefits of compounding — and of feeling financially secure about your future.

64

What happens to my 401(k) retirement plan if I change jobs?

If you wish, you can leave your 401(k) retirement plan in place at your former employer or you can roll over your retirement plan into an IRA rollover plan. In order to avoid a tax consequence, it is essential for you to roll over your 401(k) plan directly to an IRA rollover at a brokerage firm, mutual fund, or bank. If you take a distribution, twenty percent will be withheld for taxes.

65

Can I open an IRA (Individual Retirement Account) for my infant daughter?

Yes, you can open an IRA for your daughter— if she earns income. For instance, if she earns income as a child model or actress, that would be considered earned income. The amount of her earned income (up to $2,000) could be used to open an IRA, and the portion up to $2,000 would be deducted from her taxable income taxes.

Because of the benefits of compounding, opening an IRA account for children who have earned income is an excellent idea. For example, let's look at a grandparent with a grandchild who earned $2,000. If this IRA was opened when the child was 14, and every year $ 2,000 was contributed to this IRA for the next six years, the total contributions would be $12,000. Through compounding, and earning a 10% return annually, the earnings would grow tax-deferred. When that grandchild becomes 65 years old, he or she will have earned more than $1 million.

66

What do you think of senior lifecare centers for retirees?

Today's senior citizens are very different from their parents. Technological, medical, and social changes occurring during the past generation have modified the lives and expectations of senior citizens in the 1990s. When many of us were growing up, it was common to have one's grandmother living with the family. As grandmothers became widows and grandfathers became widowers, they moved in to their children's homes. This was the norm.

During the past 20-30 years, more families have become two-working-parent households. Both parents struggle to keep up with the increasing costs of living, the uncertainties caused by down-sizing or lack of job security, and galloping cost of medical services and college tuitions. These people are less able to take care of their elderly parents than prior generations were. Coupled with this dilemma, people are living much longer these days.

The major concerns of today's seniors are:
1. Maintaining their independence and not being a burden to children or spouse.
2. Outliving their savings.
3. Not being able to sustain their standard of living as they become older.
4. Not being able to drive, maintain their home, or feel safe and secure in their home.

Today's economic realities have created a need for lifecare centers for senior citizens to live in while they are healthy.

These are not nursing homes designed for those unable to care for themselves, but are adult communities that provides complete freedom for its residents. The arrangement seems to satisfy a need for companionship. The responsibilities and hassles of home-ownership are eliminated.

Since many retirees relocate to warmer climates, their children may be more than 1,000 miles away. These communities provide a way to be independent for those having the financial means and good health.

67

What should I look for when checking out the facilities of adult communities?

If you know people who are living at a community you're considering, you have an excellent source of information. Visit at different times of the day and week, talk to the residents, and ask what they like. Ask them if they had to do it over again, would they select this community? If there was anything they would like to change, what would it be?

- Find out what happens when and if health problems occur. What facilities are available? What are the costs?

- Learn about annual fees and the rate of increases for these fees.

- What transportation facilities are available when residents can no longer drive their cars?

- Examine the financial statements of the community. What kind of reputation does it have? Is it a public company? If so, have your financial consultant get a 10(k) report and annual report to analyze.

- If possible, include your children and/or grandchildren in the decision-making process. Their input may be invaluable because they may see or ask about areas that you have overlooked.

The more information you have, the more comfortable you will probably feel making a decision.

Many senior citizens, when visiting a community for the first time, say, "This is a great idea, but I'm just not ready." Once they make their move, though, they are likely to say, "I wish I had done this sooner."

Senior communities provide people with adult companionship and help eliminate anxiety about being victimized by crime or being alone when one becomes injured or ill. As baby boomers enter their 60s, these living arrangements will probably grow in popularity.

68

Why is it that some people do not purchase long term care insurance?

Many people believe that Medicare will cover their nursing home costs. The fact is Medicare pays less than 3% of these costs. It was established to provide for short-term medical attention and not intended to be used for basic care such as bathing and dressing. In rare cases that Medicare covers skilled care costs it pays only up to 100 days. In the United States, the average stay in a nursing home exceeds 450 days.

Some people think they will qualify for Medicaid coverage if they transfer their assets to family members and thereby become reduced to a state of poverty. But Medicaid has strict regulations against transferring assets to others in order to qualify for Medicaid benefits. In addition, many people would prefer not to see their life savings wasted to pay their nursing home bills.

Others do not want to face the prospect of needing long

term care insurance and deny this possibility by saying "it won't happen to me." It is estimated that approximately 50% of all Americans age 65 and over can expect to reside in a nursing home at one time or another.

69

How can I make sure that I get all of the Social Security benefits to which I'm entitled when I retire in four years?

You can request a statement listing your estimated benefits and total annual earnings. Request a "Personal Earnings and Benefits Estimate" (PEBES) form by calling 1-800-772-1213. The Social Security Administration will send it to you within one week.

70

What do you suggest that I do with my 401(k) plan distribution if my job is eliminated through downsizing?

The best option is to retain the tax-deferred status of your retirement plan by opening an IRA rollover account.

Another option is to take personal receipt of your 401(k) plan distribution and arrange to deposit these funds into your IRA. (If you choose to receive the funds directly, your former employer is required to withhold 20% for federal income tax.) You then may roll over the remaining funds (80%) into your IRA. You are required to roll over these funds within 60 days of receipt. When you file your income tax return, you then file for a refund of the 20% of your distribution withheld.

By electing the first option (a direct rollover), you will avoid the mandatory 20% withholding and have your total lump sum distribution fully invested. Approximately 70% of individuals eligible to receive a lump sum distribution because of a change or loss of jobs elect to receive these funds.

The amount received is considered income and taxed accordingly. If you are younger than 59-1/2 when you receive this distribution, there is an additional a 10% penalty.

Chapter

Understanding Equities

Investments in common stocks have proven to be the best long-term protection against inflation. Numerous convincing studies have concluded that proper asset allocation is responsible for more than 90% of the return for individual portfolios. Asset allocation is the process of determining which classes of assets to invest in. Dividend reinvestment plans are an excellent way to improve returns.

Many investors are apprehensive about the ups and downs of the stock market and want a "safer, less-risky investment." They believe the safest investments for them, as conservative investors, are insured bank accounts, CDs, and United States Treasury bills. But the fact is this: These investments are not designed for growth or inflation protection; they are secure only in that you will be guaranteed return of your principal.

Stocks usually perform better than bonds over the long run even though their value tends to fluctuate more over the course of any given week or month or year. There are various

types of stocks designed to meet the needs of all investors:
conservative, moderate and aggressive.

- **Blue-chip stocks** comprise large, well-established
  corporations that have more predictable earnings.
  Ironically, these are companies that have been reducing their work forces to try to become more globally
  competitive.
- **Growth stocks** are more volatile than blue-chips, but
  offer higher potential for appreciation.
- **Small company stocks** have the greatest risks and
  potential for appreciation.

You can offset your risk by the following:

- diversifying among several classes of stocks
- having proper asset allocation
- staying invested over the long run in spite of temporary down markets
- being diversified in your employer sponsored 403(b)
  or 401(k) plan.

Value Line and Morningstar are rating services that, respectively, publish comprehensive one-page reports on common stocks and mutual funds. These reports are usually available in your local library or from your brokerage firm.

71

What is the difference between preferred stock and regular stock?

Preferred stock and common stock are issued by companies to investors who wish to own part of the company. Preferred stock holders get preference in payment of dividends
and in case of bankruptcy or dissolution of the company. Preferred stocks normally pay a fixed interest or dividend; its price
varies inversely with interest rates. An exception is when a

preferred stock is convertible into the common stock. Then, there will be more of a direct relationship between the price of the common and the price of the preferred stock. Both preferred stock holders and common stock holders have voting rights.

72

What stocks do you recommend that I buy?

It would be presumptuous for me or any other investment advisor to recommend specific investments to you without knowing anything about you. Unless I know your personal background; your name; if you are single, married, divorced or widowed; number of dependents', your occupation, annual income and investment objectives, I couldn't begin to recommend a stock to you. In addition to making specific recommendations, I need to know your investment experience, level of expectations, the types of investments you have and your tolerance for risk. Also, what is the value of your assets? Retirement assets? Debts (including mortgages)? Is there anything unique about your situation? Any health concerns? Legal concerns? Potential inheritances or proceeds for sale of a business or practice?

Obviously if you won a $25 million lottery last year and it is payable over 20 years, your financial situation will have changed dramatically.

These are only some of the reasons why investments that are appropriate for some people are completely inappropriate for others. When a complete stranger telephones you and tries to sell you an investment without discovering first if it suits your needs, you should politely say "no thank you" and end the conversation.

73

What is the Dow Jones Average? I hear it mentioned on evening news and I don't understand it.

The Dow Jones Average is an index of 65 stocks. These 65 stocks, (30 of which are in the industrial category) are large companies such as General Electric, Coca Cola, AT&T, General Motors, DuPont, and Merck. 20 transportation stocks and 15 utility stocks are also included — for a total of 65 stocks.

The Dow Jones Industrial Average is the only price-weighted index commonly reported. This means that movements of higher-priced stock affect this average more.

The 15-stock index of the Dow Jones Utilities will give you additional insight because utilities need to borrow more heavily than to finance their capital-intensive operations. That's why this index is such an effective barometer of interest rates.

74

What are the various indices listed in the financial section of the newspaper? What do they mean?

- The most commonly quoted index is the **Dow Jones Industrial Average** (Symbol DJII). Thirty of the largest blue chip common stocks traded on the Big Board (NY Stock Exchange) comprise the Dow Jones Industrial Average.
- **The Standard & Poor 500** (S&P 500) consist of 500 blue chip stocks. The S&P 500 symbol is SPX. This is the gauge used by most portfolio managers to compare and measure their performance.
- **Dow Jones Transportation Average** (symbol DJIT) is used to track 20 large transportation common

stocks.
- **Dow Jones Utilities Average** (symbol DJIU) tracks 15 utilities stocks.
- **American Stock Exchange** (symbol AMEX) is the third largest stock exchange in the United States. This index tracks stocks on this exchange.
- **NASDAQ Composite Index** (symbol COMP) consists of smaller, usually more volatile companies traded on NASDAQ's National Market System.
- **Wilshire 5,000** (symbol WSX) offers the most comprehensive view because it tracks all major NYSE, AMEX and NASDAQ stocks.
- The index for foreign stocks is **The Morgan Stanley Capital International Europe Australia Far East Index** (EAFE). It tracks 1,080 stocks in 20 countries.

75

What stocks make up the Dow Jones Averages?

The Dow Jones Averages consist of 30 industrial companies (the Dow Jones Industrial Average), 20 transportation companies (the Dow Jones Transport Averages) and 15 utility companies (the Dow Jones Utilities Average).

The breakdown (as of 4-95) is as follows:

Industrials	Transports	Utilities
Union Carbide	Santa Fe Pacific	American Electric Power
IBM	Alaska Air	Detroit Edison
Alcoa	XTRA Corp.	Peoples Energy
Caterpillar	Consol. Freightways	Unicom Corp.
DuPont	Roadway Services	Panhandle Eastern
Coca-Cola	Delta Air Lines	Public Service Enterprise

Int'l Paper
Merck
American Express
Procter & Gamble
Boeing
Walt Disney
Eastman Kodak
Philip Morris
McDonald's
Chevron
United Tech.
Minnesota Mining
General Electric
Exxon
AT&T
Texaco
Bethlehem Steel
Sears Roebuck
Westinghouse
AlliedSignal
J.P. Morgan
General Motors
Goodyear
Woolworth

UAL Corp.
Amer. President
Norfolk Southern
CSX Corp.
Federal Express
Burlington North.
Ryder System
AMR Corp.
Conrail Inc.
Carolina Freight
Union Pacific
Airborne Freight
Southwest Airlines
US Air Group

Peco Energy
Consolidated Edison
Consolidated Natural Gas
Houston Industries
SCE Corp.
Niagara Mohawk Power
Pacific Gas & Electric
Noram Energy
Centerior Energy

76

When should I sell a stock?

    This is a common question that has no simple answer.
When to sell a stock depends upon your investment objectives.
Many people buy a stock and have no idea when they plan to
sell it. In other words, they really have no investment goal.
What happens is: the stock goes up and they don't want to sell
it because they'll have to pay capital gains tax on it. Then, the

stock starts to drop below the purchase price, causing great concern. They don't want to sell the stock then because they'll have a loss. So they decide to wait until it rises up to break-even and then at that point they plan to sell it. What happens? The stock continues to drop below the lows and reaches new lows.

For fear of paying the tax on the capital gain, these investors have missed a profit opportunity and incurred a loss.

This loss could also have been avoided through the use of a *stop loss order.* You determine at the time you purchase a stock that if it drops 10-15% below the purchase price, it is automatically sold. So, by having a selling discipline in place, you will limit your loss. As stocks starts to rise and reach new highs, you keep reestablishing your selling discipline to 15% below the new high and when it reaches that new low, the stock is automatically sold. This is one method of locking in a profit and not riding a stock without a plan.

77

What does P/E mean? I see it in the paper when I look up my stocks.

P/E stands for the price-earnings ratio. To calculate the P/E for a particular company, divide the market price of one share of stock by the annual earnings of one share of stock. For example, if the market price of a specific stock is $30 and the earnings per share are $3, then the P/E = 10.

Investors use the P/E ratio as a yardstick in evaluating a company's comparative worth. Some analysts recommend buying stocks with low P/E ratios (under 10) because it may be undervalued. It's a good idea to understand what P/E is and realize it is one of many measures to use when deciding whether to invest in a particular company.

78

What is the difference between the "bid" and "asked" prices I see in the stock quotation listings in any local newspaper?

The " bid" is the highest price an investor is willing to pay for the same security. The "asked" is the lowest price at which an investor is willing to sell a security at a specific time.

Bid and **asked** confuses many investors. To avoid confusion, rephrase them as, respectively, "What can I buy it for?" and "What can I sell it for?"

79

What is the origin of the stock market terms bear and bull?

In 18th century England, bear skin traders frequently sold their skins before they had actually caught them. "Bears" came to refer to speculators who sold shares they did not own; hoping for a price drop. They would then buy the stock after it had fallen and would immediately sell it for a higher price. **Bull** probably came to mean the opposite of **bear.**

80

Why were my utilities stocks down almost 30% from a year ago?

Utility stocks are very interest rate-sensitive. Because they borrow heavily to finance their operations as interest rates go up, the value of utility stocks tends to go down, because they have historically, paid a higher percentage of dividends than other stocks do. During the year you mentioned, there had been six increases in interest rates; that had adversely affected the value of utility stocks.

81

Florida Power and Light (FPL) cut my dividend by 34%. Is there any indicator that could have alerted me in advance? I don't have a broker.

One of the indicators that is commonly used to warn investors that a company is going to cut the dividend is that the dividend becomes greater than the earnings of the company. When the dividends of the utilities are approaching 90% or more of its earnings, that dividend may be in danger of being reduced or eliminated. This was the case with FPL.

82

How can I time the stock market just right?

Trying to time the stock market is something that you should avoid. Historically, it has been proven that individuals cannot time the stock market well. It's much more important in order to get a high return on your investments over the long term, and to have the proper asset allocation. The proper asset allocation has counted for 91% of investment returns—whereas market timing has only accounted for 2-3%.

83

Do you recommend reinvesting the dividends I receive from blue chip stocks I own?

Definitely. The return you get by reinvesting dividends is much greater than you get by receiving cash dividends.

The Standard & Poor's Composite Index of 500 widely held common stocks (commonly know as the S&P 500) has increased more than 400% during the past 15 years. If dividends from these stocks had been being reinvested in purchasing additional shares during this period, the return would have soared to 851%.

84

How do analysts evaluate a stock? How accurate are they?

Analysts evaluate stocks by examining the earnings of a company and its prospects for the future. They also analyze the prospects for growth for the industry and economy, and look at the historical data of the company's finances. They may meet with the company's management and discuss its growth and operations to get a feel for the effectiveness of its leadership. Some analysts meet with the company's competition, suppliers, customers and clients, and look for trends within the industry as well as the company. It is crucial that the analysts study the demand for the company's products or services (both domestically and overseas) so that they can accurately forecast growth prospects. In addition, they must have thorough understanding of the company's finances, profit margins, and areas for improvement.

Analysts who are not accurate in their predictions usually have to change jobs because they're replaced. Analysts stick out their necks by making forecasts and predictions, in black and white, in written reports. They are held accountable.

85

What is the difference between a limit order and market order?

A "limit order" specifies the highest price you are willing to pay for a stock, or the lowest price you will accept for the sale of a stock you own.

If you make a "market order," you are not specifying a price; your order will be executed for the best price available at the time you place the order. You'll learn the price after the order has been executed.

86

What is the difference between "technical analysis" and "fundamental analysis" in evaluating stocks?

Fundamental analysis studies the basics of a company's finances and its economic prospects before making a decision to buy, hold, or sell its stock. Fundamental analysis studies a company's prime earnings ratios, dividend history, rate of return, sales, and profitability history and trends.

Technical analysis uses past and current stock price movements to predict future prices of a company's stock. It relies heavily on charts to plot the price movement of stocks. No consideration is given to any of the components used in fundamental analysis.

87

What are defensive stocks?

Defensive stocks are stocks that are less vulnerable to the swings of the business cycle than most other stocks tend to be. Some defensive stocks include utilities, tobacco and food stocks. They are considered defensive because consumers need to buy these products or services regardless of changes in their personal incomes or job situation.

88

Should I invest in retail company stocks?

Your question is very general and, while there are many dynamic retail corporations, there are also retailers who have either been unable to find their markets or have lost them.

An excellent way to judge retail sales is to make a "same-store sales comparison." To do this, you need to compare sales at stores that have been open for at least one year. By looking only at stores that have been open for a year or more, you eliminate the effects of increased sales caused by recent new store openings.

When analyzing a manufacturing company, use comparative unit sales rather than dollar sales to get a better indicator of demand for the company's products.

Chapter

Understanding Bonds

Many investors view bonds and bond mutual funds as conservative investments that provide a steady income and represent a minimal risk to principal. That's because if you hold your bond until maturity, you get the full amount of your investment *plus* interest. (A bond is an obligation of its issuer to pay the interest and principal as promised.)

Zero-coupon bonds are very popular among parents and grandparents who are funding a child's education. A zero-coupon bond is issued at a discount from its par value (or face value). It only pays interest with principal at maturity or at the time the bond is called. Unlike other types of bonds, interest on zero-coupon bonds is not paid to you every six months; it is automatically reinvested or compounded at the agreed-upon rate at time of purchase. The combination of compounding and the discounted price means that a relatively small investment can multiply significantly before the bond matures. The longer the maturity length of the bond, the deeper the discount usually is.

In addition to being used to fund a college education, zero-coupon bonds appeal to many individual investors who are planning for retirement. If placed in SEPs, IRAs or Keoghs, they are not subject to immediate taxation since these accounts are tax-deferred. By making an investment in a zero-coupon bond today, investors know exactly how much they will receive at maturity.

Municipal bonds are debt securities issued by public authorities (such as states or municipalities) to raise funds for building or repairing schools, highways, prisons, bridges, tunnels and other public works. The interest payments you receive on municipal bonds is free from federal income taxes. The higher your tax bracket, the more you will benefit by investing in "munis" and earning tax-free income.

If you live in a high income tax state you may also derive additional benefits from owning in-state bonds that are also state income tax-exempt.

Interest on bonds issued by the U.S. Virgin Islands, Guam and the Commonwealth of Puerto Rico are exempt from federal, state and local taxes in all fifty states.

Corporate bonds complement many investment portfolios—especially retirement accounts and accounts with low marginal tax rates.

Many reputable companies raise capital by issuing **corporate bonds** to purchase or update equipment, build plants, and replace outstanding debt with lower cost issues. Credit rating agencies such as Moody's and Standard & Poor's (S&P) study the creditworthiness of the issuer of the bond, and assign a rating to that bond as a general guideline for investors.

Investment grade ratings used by agencies are:

Moody's	S&P
Aaa	AAA
Aa	AA
A	A
Baa	BBB

These agencies revise their ratings when they feel the creditworthiness of an issue changes.

United States government securities are among the most secure of all income-producing investments. They are available in two forms: direct obligations of the U. S. government and those issued by various agencies which are indirect obligations of the U.S. government.

All bonds (U.S. Treasuries, federal agencies, zero-coupons, corporates and municipals) are subject to market fluctuations if you sell them before they mature. Investing in bonds has become more complex in recent years as the choice of taxable and tax-exempt bonds has expanded and volatility in bond prices and interest rates has increased.

89

How do bonds work?

When a bond is issued by a corporation or a municipality, it is sold at face value. The investor usually pays $1,000 per bond. The par value also includes the amount that will be redeemed or repaid at maturity.

To calculate the market price of a bond, use the following formula:

current yield = amount of coupon / market price

If a 6% bond is issued at par or $1,000, the amount of coupon interest = $60

$$.06 = \$60 / \$1000$$

When the Federal Reserve raises interest rates to 8% in order to reduce inflationary pressures, the market price is reduced as follows:

current yield = amount of coupon/market price

current yield = .08
coupon (remains constant)= $60
market price = X

$.08 = \$60/X$; $.08\,X = \$60$; $X = \$60/.08$; $X = \$750$ market price

When interest rates are lowered, the market price of a bond increases. Let's assume the Federal Reserve lowers interest rates from 6% to 5% to stimulate the economy. The effect of the market price is as follows:

current yield = amount of coupon/market price

current yield = .05
coupon = $60

$$.05 = \$60/X \qquad X = \$1,200 \text{ market price}$$

90

I'm 68 years old and I understand the benefit of investing in insured tax-free municipal bonds. But are there any disadvantages?

Yes, there are three disadvantages; market risk, inflation risk and call risk. The principal of these bonds is only guaranteed upon maturity.

- If you wish to sell them prior to maturity and interest rates have gone up considerably since you've purchased them, you will find that the principal is less than the purchase price, and you will be taking a loss if you sell them. This is market risk.
- If you hold tax-free bonds until maturity, the money you get back (even though it is equal to the face-value of the bonds) has lost purchasing power over the years because of inflation. Bonds that you've held for thirty years may only have 25% of the purchasing power they had when you purchased them. This is inflation risk.
- When interest rates drop, the issuer of your bonds may wish to call or redeem them and refinance them at a lower rate. This is call risk.

91

How can I know whether I'm better off investing in tax-able or tax-free bonds?

By computing whether the return net of taxes is greater than tax-free versus tax or vice versa. How do you do this? There is a formula for computing the tax equivalent. Take your tax-free return percentage-wise, divide it by one minus your income tax bracket. That will give you the tax equivalent. Let's assume somebody has a six percent tax-free investment and is in the forty percent tax bracket. Put 6% in the numerator and then (1-.40) in the denominator (so you have .06/.60). The answer is .10 or 10%. So, the 6% tax free bond would be the equivalent of 10% before taxes (if an investor is in the 40% bracket).

$$\text{Tax Equivalent Yield (TEY)} = \frac{\text{Tax-free return}}{1 - \text{income tax bracket}}$$

$$\text{TEY} = \frac{.06}{1 - .40}$$

$$\text{TEY} = \frac{.06}{.60}$$

$$\text{TEY} = .1 \text{ or } 10\%$$

92

Is there any risk associated with investing in CDs?

CDs (certificates of deposit) are insured by the Federal Deposit Insurance Corporation (FDIC). There is no risk of default on the principal of a CD, but there is risk that the value of the CD will diminish through loss of purchasing power. Remember, the only true value money has is the value of the items it can buy. If the value of the items an investment can buy is reduced, then there is a risk of inflation. Many retirees are frustrated when their CDs or bonds come due and the amount of purchasing power has been reduced by inflation.

93

Is there a rating service for bonds (similar to Morningstar Ratings for mutual funds and Value Line for stocks)?

There are three rating services: Moodys, Standard & Poor's and Fitch. The highest rating is AAA, then AA, A , BBB, BB and B for investment grade quality. When a municipality pays to insure their bonds, their credit rating is enhanced and becomes AAA.

94

What are mortgage-backed bonds?

Mortgage-backed bonds or collateralized mortgage obligations (CMOs) are pools of mortgages repurchased by the agencies that issue them. Some of these agencies are better known by their nicknames:

- **Ginnie Mae** stands for Government National Mortgage Association (GNMA)
- **Freddie Mac** stands for Federal Home Loan Mortgage Corporation (FHLMC)
- **Fannie Mae** stands for Federal National Mortgage Association (FNMA)

Each payment the investor receives is for interest only until the return of principal payments begin.

95

What is a money-market account? How does it differ from an account at a bank? Can you write checks against it?

A money-market account is not *guaranteed* by the brokerage firm from which you buy it. There is no fluctuation of principal. The interest rate is, in almost all cases, considerably higher than is found at a bank. Many brokerage firms offer accounts that enable owners to write checks against their account.

96

Am I better off investing in registered or book-entry municipal bonds? Can you purchase the same bond either way? Is there a price difference?

Most municipal bonds are issued in book-entry form only. You are probably better off buying book-entry municipal bonds because, that way, you will not have to worry about losing your certificates. A bond cannot be purchased both in book-entry and registered form. They are only issued in one form or the other.

97

I am retired and have recently changed my residence from New York to Florida. Does it make sense for me to "swap" or exchange my New York municipal bonds for Florida ones?

Compare your New York municipal bonds with those available in Florida, and see if the return justifies the swap. If your return in New York is equal to your potential return on a Florida bond, then the additional Florida Intangible Tax may make it worthwhile for you to "swap" into Florida municipal bonds.

98

What is a callable bond?

When interest rates drop, an issuer (such as a corporation or municipality) may wish to redeem its outstanding bonds and refinance them at a lower rate. It's similar to an individual refinancing a home mortgage when interest rates drop considerably since the date the mortgage was issued. Bonds with call provisions protect investors from having their bonds called or redeemed before a specified date (such as 5 or 10 year call protection).

99

What does "laddering a portfolio" mean?

"Laddering" is a strategy for protection against interest rate risk when buying tax-free or taxable bonds that have different maturities. Think of a portfolio with bonds that have varying maturities as resembling rungs of a ladder. By purchasing bonds that mature at set intervals, the investor has diversified in case of changes in interest rates. In addition the investor can plan for income and reinvest principal at set intervals.

100

On cable TV they talk a lot about the yield curve being normal or inverted. What does this mean and why is it important?

A yield curve is a graph that plots interest rates for a security that is issued with different maturity lengths. Yield curves can be plotted for municipal bonds, corporate bonds and treasury securities. (Interest rate is measured on the vertical axis and the time period on the horizontal axis.)

The yield curve that is generally referred to on TV is the yield curve for Treasury securities. It usually slopes upward because interest rates are higher as maturity lengths increase. This is what is called a "positive" or "normal" yield curve.

When short-term interest rates shoot up because of inflation fears, the yield curve slopes downward because longer-term maturities have lower rates. The yield curve in this scenario is called "inverted."

In rare instances, short-term and long-term interest rates are almost equal. The yield curve is then called "flat."

101

What does "secondary market" mean?

After a stock is issued in an initial public offering (referred to as an "IPO"), its shares may be sold and bought again and again. The "again and again" constitutes the secondary market.

102

Does a T-bill differ from a treasury note? A treasury bond? or are they all the same?

A T-bill (Treasury bill) is a short-term obligation of the U.S. Government. They have maturity lengths of one year or less, are purchased at a discount and mature at face value. At maturity (either 13, 26, or 52 weeks), the difference between your purchase price and maturity value is considered taxable interest income.

Treasury notes and Treasury bonds are also U.S. Government obligations but have longer maturities. The maturities are:
- Treasury notes: 2-10 years
- Treasury bonds: more than 10-30 years

Both Treasury notes and Treasury bonds pay interest every six months and are issued in $1,000 denominations.

When financial broadcasters refer to the interest of the "long bond," they mean the 30-year U.S. Treasury bond.

Chapter

Paying For College

In the last twenty years, the cost of a college education has increased at more than double the rate
of inflation. In some Ivy League schools, alumni children are
literally paying more for one semester's tuition than their parents paid for four year's tuition thirty years ago.

If you start an educational funding investment plan when
your child or grandchild is an infant, it will be much less of a
strain on your finances. To begin formulating your investment
plan, you need to calculate how much it will cost and how
much you will need to invest (either in one lump sum or annually). Most major brokerage firms have computer programs
designed to determine the cost for college educations for up to
four children in a family. These programs usually have a selection of 1,700 or so colleges and universities, their associated four-year costs and historic annual increases.

A growing number of people have postponed starting a
family until they were in their 40s. Instead of funding their

retirement plans, they are now paying college bills and may also be providing support for elderly parents.

Although it can represent a financial challenge to fund a child's education, most people realize the importance of doing so: studies have shown that a college education can help boost lifetime income by $1 million.

103

What investments do you recommend for funding a college education?

A lot depends upon the age of the people involved. The proper investment needs to be determined by the time horizon and the risk tolerance of the investor. If the future college student is one or two years away from entering college, then the time horizon is quite short. You would have less risk investing in more liquid investments with less volatility so that the principal would be available in the next one or two years when the money is needed.

If a child is five years or more away from entering college, you will want this investment to have more growth benefits and would therefore likely select either a mutual fund, common stocks, or even a zero-coupon bond. You may wish to use investments that have a lot of volatility and a minimum of a four to five year cycle.

104

I am worried about being able to afford to pay for a college education for my children (ages 3 and 5). How can I estimate the costs and be able to pay for them?

The first part of your question deals with estimating the costs of a four-year college education for your two children starting in thirteen and fifteen years, respectively. We know the approximate current costs of a four-year college for a private college, state university, and expensive private colleges. Based upon the past, we can also estimate the annual increase for tuition and room and board. College costs have increased at more than twice the rate of the Consumer Price Index. Based upon this increase, I would estimate the annual increase at 8%.

To calculate an estimate, let's assume college costs (tuition, room and board, and other expenses) are $6,500 at a public college. An easy way to compute this is to use a pocket calculator that has a memory. First, put 1.08 into the memory (to reflect the total amount of tuition each year including the annual increase of 8%). Then multiply the starting cost of $6,500 times memory recall (MR) or 1.08 and that will give you the total cost in 13 and 15 years by pressing MR 13 and 15 times. Remember, this is a rough estimate because we're relying only upon historical data.

105

Is there a way for me to pay for my grandson's college education without having to pay the gift tax? His tuition costs more than $10,000 yearly.

Yes. We know that the annual gift tax exclusion per person is limited to $10,000, but we also know that the annual cost of college can be $20,000-30,000.

If you pay this tuition by giving your grandson the money, and then he pays the tuition, you will have a gift tax obligation. But you can legally circumvent the $10,000 gift tax limitation by paying your grandson's college tuition directly to the university or college.

But this does not cover the costs for room and board and transportation. If you wish to pay for your grandson's room and board and transportation costs, this will come out of the $10,000 gift tax exclusion.

In the same way, you can pay for someone's medical expenses or hospital expenses by paying the medical provider (whether it's a hospital or doctor) directly. That way, if the bill comes to more than $10,000, and you pay it directly you have a non-gift tax event. This is one of the rare instances that the IRS allows us to have our cake and eat it too.

106

Are pre-paid college tuition plans a good investment? Did I do the right thing by enrolling my two children in the Florida Prepaid Tuition Plan?

That depends upon certain factors. Currently, seven states (including Florida) have prepaid college tuition plans. (Others are Alaska, Kentucky, Ohio, Michigan, Alabama, and Wyoming) The Florida Prepaid Tuition Plan is an excellent way for parents and grandparents to provide for a child's college education. Without these plans, many of the families would not be able to provide a college education for their children.

The Florida Prepaid College Tuition Plan covers the cost for tuition and room and board at Florida public universities, colleges, and junior colleges. It does not cover the cost of tuition at private universities in Florida, or at public universities and colleges outside of the state of Florida.

What would happen if your two children who are enrolled in the Florida Prepaid Tuition Plan decide to go to college outside of Florida or at a private university within Florida (such as the University of Miami)? They'll receive either 1) a refund that is equal to the amount of money put into the plan plus 5% annual increases, or 2) the cost of tuition currently at a Florida public university (whichever is less).

It's safe to say that you could have probably received a much better return over the long run than 5%. The cost of college tuition has increased at approximately double the Consumer Price Index (CPI) 8-10%. If you had known that your children were planning to go to an out-of-state university, you would have been better off investing in a growth mutual fund. In that case, the Florida Prepaid Tuition Plan was definitely not a good investment. However, if your children plan to go to college in Florida and you want to lock in the cost of tuition increases, this can be an excellent investment.

Chapter 8

Insurance and Taxes

Taxes and inflation reduce your real rate of re-turn. Together, they can destroy an investor's dream of providing a college education for children, buying a home for the family or enjoying a comfortable retirement.

By using tax-deferred investments such as IRAs, SEPs, annuities and 401(k) / 403(b) plans; your investments are able to compound faster over time.

Protect your earning power by having disability insurance, and protect your assets from being depleted to pay nursing home care costs by having long term care insurance.

107

How much life insurance should I buy?

The amount of life insurance you should buy depends upon

your current assets and your financial obligations.

In rare cases (such as in the case of people who are very wealthy and have everything they need), a person may require no insurance to provide protection for his family. Many wealthy individuals buy life insurance policies to provide funds to pay their estate taxes. Most people with young children need insurance so that these children will be provided for until they're adults.

How much life insurance do you need? That's usually a compromise between the amount of money that you are able to afford and the amount of insurance protection you need. Usually very young people with small children and limited means can maximize the amount of life insurance by buying term insurance so that their children and spouse are protected.

You may have heard the story about the carpenter who had only one tool: a hammer. He saw every problem or opportunity as a nail. If you ask a full time life insurance agent how much life insurance you should buy, you'll probably get a much different answer from mine.

108

What do you recommend I do to reduce the amount of taxes I have to pay?

Some tax planning strategies that taxpayers use to legally reduce the amount of their tax bill include:

- Invest in tax-free investments like municipal bonds. Interest income from these bonds is exempt from federal income tax, and may also be exempt from state and local income taxes.

- Use a home equity loan to finance major expenses

such as college education and home remodeling. Interest expenses for home equity loans are tax deductible even if that home is not your primary residence.

- Pay expenses with pre-tax dollars rather than after-tax dollars, if your employer offers flexible spending and a 401(k) or 403(b) retirement plan. Non-profit organizations offer 403(b) plans.

- Shift income and deductions from one year to the next to achieve a reduced taxable income level. For example, only medical expenses that are deductible are those that exceed 7.5% of income. You may be in a position to schedule elective surgery so that it falls within the year when your medical expenses exceed 7.5%.

- Rather than making cash donations to charities, donate appreciated assets. By doing this you avoid the capital gains tax on the appreciated portion and are permitted to deduct the total amount of your donation. For example, if a stock originally bought for $200 has grown in value to $1,000, then when you sold it for $1,000, you would have $800 in gain subject to the current capital gains tax. However, if you donated this stock (worth $1,000) to a legitimate charity, you would have no tax liability and would be eligible for a $1,000 deduction from your income tax.

- Sell securities with a loss to offset securities already sold with a gain.

- Contribute up to $ 2,000 to an Individual Retirement Account (IRA) if you are not covered by a retirement plan at work. This amount should increase to $2,250

if you have a non-working spouse. The amount of
the IRA contribution is deducted from your taxable
income.

• Investing in tax deferred investments (such as annuities) permits earnings in subsequent years to grow
faster because they are not subject to income taxes
— as long as they are sheltered in that annuity. Earnings accrue tax-deferred until they are redeemed.

109

**Should I buy long term care insurance now? Or wait until
I'm 65?**

Yes, buy long term care insurance. If you don't buy this
insurance and become ill and uninsurable, you will have taken
an unnecessary risk. Let's look at the real cost of waiting by
examining and comparing the real cost for a benefit if an individual enrolls at age 55 versus enrolling at a later age.

The $100 benefit at age 55 will increase (due to inflation-
ary pressure) to $130 in five years and to $170 in ten years.
The total cost is much less if this policy is purchased at age 55.
Aside from the economic benefits, think of the peace of mind
you'll have knowing that your assets will not be depleted to
pay for your long term care.

110

Should I buy flood insurance? I own my home free and clear and don't have a mortgage company or bank requiring me to buy flood insurance.

If you live in a flood-or earthquake-prone area, you need to buy the proper insurance or be prepared to face the consequences of being uninsured.

Before Hurricane Andrew struck south Florida in August 1992, many retirees who had paid off their mortgages had no longer been required to carry flood insurance. These retirees felt that the cost for these premiums was an escapable cost because it had been about 30 years since the last destructive hurricane. Some of these uninsured homeowners in Homestead and South Miami suffered massive damage and lost their uninsured homes.

Many homeowners purchased insurance policies that paid only depreciated costs — not replacement costs. A 10-year old couch that originally cost $1,000 depreciates to $100, and its replacement cost is $1,500. How much will an insurance company reimburse even if the couch is totally destroyed? For a replacement cost policy, insurance will pay $1,500. For a depreciated cost policy, it will only pay $100.

111

What is an annuity?

An annuity is a contract sold by an insurance company to an individual. It provides payments to the purchaser (usually during retirement).

By investing in annuities, 100% of your money works for you because you receive both interest earned and interest on the portion that would have gone for taxes.

A **fixed annuity** earns a set rate of return. A **variable-rate annuity** earnings fluctuates depending upon the value of the investments.

If you cash in an annuity before 59-1/2, you incur the same penalties as you would have if you had cashed an IRA in before age 59-1/2: 10% penalty plus income taxes owed.

Think of a variable annuity as a mutual fund that is permitted to grow tax-sheltered. You do not receive an annual 1099 form on the earnings of your variable annuity. You pay taxes when you decide to receive this money. You are not required to receive a certain distribution amount at age 70-1/2 as you would be with an IRA.

112

Do I need to have disability insurance?

Disability insurance pays you a monthly income if you become unable to work as a result of sickness or injury. It is estimated that a 40-year old is four times more likely to become disabled than to die. However, most 40-year olds with life insurance coverage are not protected by disability insurance.

The premium for your disability insurance policy is determined by your age, sex, occupation, medical history and the amount of coverage desired. Those in certain occupations are required to pay a higher premium; those in others (such as law enforcement) are usually not insurable.

More expensive disability policies are usually noncancelable. Insurance companies define "disabled" as not being able to perform your own occupation and not having any related occupation.

113

What is a deferred annuity and how does it differ from CDs, bonds, and mutual funds?

Banks issue CDs, corporations or governments issue bonds, investment companies issue mutual funds, and insurance companies issue tax-deferred annuities.

A tax-deferred annuity is a contract with an insurance company with whom you invest a specific amount of money — either in one lump sum or periodically. At a future date of choice (usually after you retire), you start to withdraw the money. You select a plan that allows you to stipulate the amount and frequency of your income distributions.

114

My company offers a flex-spending medical benefits program and I haven't enrolled because I was told if I don't use the amount deducted I lose it. Can you explain this?

Flexible spending accounts are offered usually by large corporations as part of employee health benefit programs. It enables members to use pre-tax dollars to pay for medical and/or child care or dependent expenses. Medical expenses that are not covered by health insurance (because of deductibles, co-payments, or because such items excluded such as dental prescription glasses, contact lenses, braces, and some other expenses) are covered by flexible spending accounts.

What you are doing is using flexible pre-tax income to pay for items that would normally be paid using after-tax income.

Chapter

Wills

It is estimated that two thirds of American adults do not have wills, forcing the state or courts to appoint guardians for their minor children and decide who will receive their assets after their death.

Many people fail to prepare wills because it is easier to postpone a seemingly unpleasant task than face the reality of their mortality. We have a basic conflict in our society: when asked, most people say they want to go to heaven but they also don't want to die.

By preparing a will, you will ensure that your personal goals are met for the disposition of your assets. Your peace of mind is your immediate reward.

115

What is meant by "probate"?

A probate proceeding validates your will before a court. It is used to determine whether you really signed your will and whether you were competent at that time to do so.

116

What are the costs of probate?

As a general rule-of-thumb, many estate planners estimate that 5% of the value of assets cover the costs for executor, attorney, appraiser and accountants fees.

117

Can I avoid probate?

Some methods used to avoid probate include:

- Hold your assets in joint tenancy. The ownership of the assets passes automatically to the surviving joint tenant.
- Life insurance that is not payable to an estate generally bypasses probate administration (but not estate taxes).
- Revocable living trusts protect the assets in that trust from being subjected to probate administration at time of death. This saves executor and attorney fees, and offers privacy about inheritances.
- Gifts made before death avoid probate.

118

How much will I need to pay in federal estate taxes?

Federal estate taxes apply only to estates that are valued in excess of $600,000. This tax increases progressively from 37% to 55% on estates greater than $3,000,000. There is a 5% surcharge on estates between $10-$21,000,000.

119

When must estate taxes be paid? May tangible assets (such as real estate) be used to pay them?

Estate taxes must generally be paid in cash within nine months of death. If market conditions are less than favorable, a forced sale could result in severe financial sacrifice.

120

What information should I leave for my heirs in addition to my will?

You may wish to leave a special letter of instruction for them, as well as a farewell letter explaining your wishes and giving advice to your loved ones.

You may also wish to include instructions to help them wrap up your personal affairs (such as the location of important documents, tax returns, safe deposit boxes, credit cards, outstanding loans, social security number, military honorable discharge papers, special details about your personal effects, property deeds, or matters pending litigation). This is an excellent way for you to tie up any loose ends. Any preferences you have regarding funeral and burial arrangements can be communicated in this letter.

Your letter of instruction is an excellent way to say goodbye to those you love.

121

Are life insurance proceeds included in computing estate taxes?

Yes. Life insurance proceeds are used in computing estate taxes. However, proceeds not payable to an estate generally bypass probate administration. If a life insurance policy is structured so that the insured is not the owner, then the policy benefits may be excluded from estate taxes. You need to consult with a competent estate attorney to ensure your policy is structured properly.

122

If I have a joint account (with rights of survivorship) with my adult daughter and I funded the account, do I need her signature on a stock certificate in order to sell it?

Even though all the money in this account was deposited by you, you still need your daughter's signature to sell any stock held in that account. If you and your daughter owned a home jointly and you decided to sell it, both of your signatures would be required. The same principle holds true for ownership of securities in joint accounts.

Chapter **10**

Home Ownership

Buying a home used to be the largest single investment confronting most people. Many baby boomers have discovered that paying for private college educations for their two or three children has eclipsed the cost of purchasing their home. When these same individuals calculate the amount they need to invest for a comfortable retirement that is likely to span thirty plus years, they are shocked to discover it exceeds the combined costs of paying for their home and their children's college educations.

Because of these conflicting demands, some people have decided to rent rather then buy homes and invest what they save in growth mutual funds and seek to obtain a greater return on their money.

Hundreds of years ago—before the industrial revolution and the existence of factories—people worked out of their homes. Now again, in the information and telecommunications age, many Americans no longer work in downtown or suburban office complexes. They are able to work at home, linked to the workplace by computers, modems, and faxes. We seem to be going full circle.

123

Is buying a house as a sound investment strategy?

Buying a home is an excellent idea — if you plan to make that home your primary residence. This should be the reason you buy a house — not because it's a good investment.

Home prices usually increase at the rate of inflation. Many home buyers have had trouble selling their homes at a profit during the last four years. The federal government encourages Americans to own their own homes by making interest payments for mortgages and property tax payments tax deductible.

124

How can I save on my mortgage?

There are several ways to save on your mortgage if you are willing and able (unlike most homeowners) to pay more in the near term to realize major savings in the long term.

By paying your loan over 15 years instead of 30 years you'll save considerably. Your monthly payments will be approximately 30% more, but you'll wipe out your debt in half the time. Some lenders charge 1/4 to 1/2% less for a 15-year mortgage.

Another way is to prepay your mortgage (if there is no penalty for doing so). If your lender permits you to pay your mortgage every two weeks, you'll pay half the monthly amount every two weeks. In the course of one year, that totals 26 payments (26 x 1/2 = 13) or 13 months. Under this plan, your 30-year mortgage will be paid off in 23-24 years.

125

Do you recommend applying for a fixed- or variable-rate mortgage for my primary residence?

The answer to this question depends upon where you plan to live, your ability to make the mortgage payments and cover your closing costs. If you plan to move within a short time and interest rates are low, a variable rate mortgage is probably best. If interest rates are low and you lock in a fixed-rate mortgage at that low rate, then as interest rates start to go up, your low rate will not be raised.

On the other hand, consider whether your annual income is likely to increase significantly? If so, you are in a better position of affording increased monthly mortgage payments in later years.

126

Do you think I should invest in raw land?

Without knowing anything about your portfolio, your risk tolerance and your investment objectives, it would be unwise for any financial advisor to advise you. Raw land is a real estate investment that offers no benefit from either income or depreciation. It only offers the benefit of possible appreciation.

Real estate, however, can be one of many investments in a diversified portfolio. We've heard stories of individuals investing in raw land that suddenly multiplies in value when oil or some precious mineral is discovered on it, or when a major shopping center developer purchases it.

127

How can I make sure my credit reports are accurate? Can I get a copy of my own credit report.

Yes. I suggest you check your credit report yearly because mistakes can and do occur. In addition, stolen or unauthorized use of credit cards and charge cards can damage your credit rating. Also, mistakes are caused by confusion created by individuals with the same name.

To order your credit report, you can call any of these three major credit reporting agencies toll-free.

- TRW (800-392-1122)
- TransUnion (800-851-2674)
- Equifax (800-685-1111)

Index

Contact Author Form
Questions and Comments

Fax: (954) 561-6569

Write: Steven Camp
                P. O. Box 11779
                Fort Lauderdale, Florida 33339-9930

Telephone: (954) 561-6515

My questions and/or comments are:

_____

_____

_____

_____

_____

_____

Your Name _____

Address _____

City _____ State _____ Zip _____

Telephone _____

(Please photocopy)

Order Form

Telephone Orders: Call 1 (800) 356-9315

Please have your American Express, Discover, Visa or Mastercard ready.

Postal Orders: Trunkey Publishing Company
2841 NE 21 Court
Fort Lauderdale, FL 33305-3617

Please send *MONEY: 127 Answers to Your Most-Asked Financial Questions*

Company Name: _____

Name_____

Address _____

City _____ State _____ ZIP _____

Telephone (_____) _____

Shipping:
Book rate $2.00 for the first book and 75 cents for each additional book (Surface shipping may take three to four weeks)

Air Mail: $3.50 per book

Payment:
Send check payable to Trunkey Publishing Company.

Call Toll-Free and order now.

(Please photocopy)